The Rivers of My Need

The Rivers of My Need

by

PEGGY ASTON

ISBN 1-58500-410-3

1stBooks – Rev. 3/3/00

About the Book

Two rivers merge at Peggy's birthplace, Paducah, Kentucky. One clear, the other muddy, together they typify two of life's strongest emotions...joy and heartache. Thus, the book was named **The Rivers of My Need**.

...portraying the "Needs" we have for our Roots, for Belonging, for Giving and Receiving Love, for Laughter, Tears and Values,
....which are the result of the "Emotions" we Feel, as we Journey - like a Winding River - through Life.

For a Refreshing Return to Rhyming Verse.....the Collection consists of 9 Chapters (70 poems) on the following themes:

Historical, Day-to-Day (Optimistic and Humorous), Friendship, Motivational & Inspirational, Children's, Romance (all shades of Love), Spiritual and Tribute to Princess Diana.

The Rivers of My Need.....is intended to be cozy armchair reading, to "touch" the reader through Poetry Portraits of the Past, Present and Future. At times reflective, sometimes light and uplifting, always touching us amidst varying emotional levels on life experiences of our society.

The Rivers of My Need

Table of Contents

Chapter Outline

American Heritage - Great Bird in the Sky looks to the past for insight into the present and future, taking us back to the early American Indian, so adaptable and comfortable with Mother Earth, and contrasts their life through a "vision" with the jet plane and the jet-pace we live today...yet showing the similarities in our everyday lives and how we still lose ourselves and our problems in the frivolity of dancing and gaiety...which brings us to **There's Going to be a Square Dance Tonight. My Desert Storm Hero** and **War and Peace** remind us that all through time there have been wars around the globe, and how much we're willing to give to achieve freedom, even for others. **Replicas of Days Gone By** revisits life of a child in early 1900's....**The Call of Long Ago** takes a nostalgic walk around an early settlement community, and you can almost hear the horses hooves on bridges of wooden planks.

Day-by-Day, a Reflection (Optimistic) - Age deals with the young-at-heart and aging gracefully...**Dreams** allows us to still do so...**Only a Year** gives eternal hope for terminal illness...**See the Old House** is a return to the old homestead, standing in the field...over there...shall we step inside? **Seventeen Winters Ago** remembers the reasons why we had our children...**Survival** achieves success for the woman who has met the challenges of Corporate America... **The Seasons of Our Lives** takes a look at life through the eyes of a blind person...**You're a Star**...for the shining star in your life.

Day-by-Day, a Reflection (Humorous) - All in a Day's Work is the typical day in the life of a mother and child....**Daddy, When Can I Drive** reveals Bobby's strong desire to drive Dad's car, as a little boy, to age 16 and Prom Night...**Double X Lex** on fleeting boyhood....**Garage Sale Fever** shows there's a little bargain hunter in all of us. **Let's Go Out for Dinner Tonight** explores all the neat places to dine out, with an unexpected ending. **Payday Blues** typifies the family on payday. **That Horse will Win Someday** puts us at the sidelines of a horse-race...**Your Charming Rabbit Hat** captures a successful shopping trip.

The Friendship Flower - Char's Legacy explores the timeless, inner beauty of a dear friend...**Coffee Klatch** finds two gals gleefully gossiping over coffee...**My Favorite Man** attempts to give Dad credit... **My Golf Man** is for the golfer from the golf-widow...**My Mother the Lady** pays homage to our role model...**My Precious Friend**, for the one who has been there when we thought there was no one to care...**Only a Fortnight Ago** is the return to the highschool reunion and old feelings.. **The Friendship Flower** likens friends to a colorful bouquet... **The Lady Manager,** offers a shining example in today's busy business world....and **The Man in the Brown Business Suit** pays tribute to a respected man.

Superior Force Collection - Take 2 Minutes and **Dream Dynastyland** were written on request to be a source of inspiration for the recovering alcoholic. **The Passage of Time** offers encouragement, and **Time In** recognizes sobriety anniversary.

On the Way to the Treestump Tea Party - A Happy Yesterday is a ploy for discipline in child...**Hobo, the Cross-Eyed Cat** shows just now lovable the family pet really is... **On the Way to the Treestump Tea Party** brings our furry friends of the forest to lifelike animation... **The Alphabet Love Story -** takes us from A to Z as the child grows up.

In the Village Chapel - paints all shades of love...**Belated Roses** is a new twist with the lady doing the apologizing... **Blue Days of Regret -** have blue days of regret overtaken you?.. **Daughter of Miine** reflects on the strong bond between women of three generations. In **Dreams I'm Afraid to Speak** the lady is typically holding back her feelings... **In the Village Chapel** the youthful couple marry amidst skepticism, only to return to the chapel for their 50th Anniversary while hosts of angels sang... **Johnnie, Can You Hear Me?** she loves him beyond flesh but God loves them more... **Leave Me if You Need To** a woman's fears realized...in **Man of My Dreams** she makes us all jealous of her good fortune... **My Fondest Dream** expresses woman's innermost feelings when asked by the man in her life.... **On Beyer's Old 4th Floor** on the cycle of life.....**Opportunity was Her Name** contrasts the Lady in Red with the Lady in Black.... in **The Arms that Once Held Me** she struggles with him wanting to leave her...**The Low Road** deals with separation/divorce recovery optimistically... **The Rivers of My Need** in esteem of true love... **The Stranger** depicts the man with a roving eye... **The Sunshine Ship** is as near as a sigh to the Isle of Love.

King of Kings - Faith Speaking Collection - Are You Really a Christian, Did you Know Jesus, the Child.....the Man... the Saviour ...**The Single Man's and Woman's Prayers** are in support of morality and are spiritually uplifting... **Does God Need Another Soprano** shows that only one can make a difference.....**The Talks We Used to Share** on prayer...**Where is God?** finds God to be anywhere we are... **Who Made Man, Perfect Man**, would you care to try, not I.

Tribute to Princess Diana - The Pearl portrays the inner beauty of the Queen of Hearts, reflecting on the qualities that "lift" her above physical beauty, to remain in our hearts forever....**The Roses** speaks for the heartache of many.

Chapter 1

American Heritage
Collection

MY DESERT STORM HERO

My Love, as I write to you tonight,
Knowing you have "given" with all your might,
Please know I miss and love you so.
You are my Desert Storm Hero.

The Hard Work of Freedom was never for the weak.
For this noble cause you so bravely stand and speak.
May the land held hostage be unbound and released
Through a Power from above, rushing in on Wings of Peace.

Remember the *RED*
　　for the Hardiness and Courage of women and men
　　who have stood tall for Freedom time and again

Remember the *WHITE*
　　may it always signify the Purity and Innocence
　　of a nation, harmless in Intention and Blameless

Remember the *BLUE*
　　without it we would have just left things to chance,
　　for it stands for Perseverance and Vigilance

These high standards, the vital elements of Peace . . . . .
Without them, can there truly be any relief?
The tie that binds us is even stronger for these demands.
America's prayers for Desert Storm outnumber the sand!

The meaning of the Flag was
researched for a greater message.

REPLICAS OF DAYS GONE BY

What would I Give you for Your Birthday, if Only I
    Could?

Definitely a Bouquet of Red Roses, from my Garden,
And, Oh Yes, a Giant, Life-Size Birthday Card.
Maybe even a Set of Fine, China Dishes would
    Magically Appear,
And a Wishing Well of Warm Wishes for what you
    hold Most Dear.

Perhaps a Bright, Beautiful Day to Relive as a Child,
Playing in Country Fields, in Summer, Sunny and
    Mild.
Quietly Reading, or Playing your Favorite Game,
And a 1920's Stroll down Memory Lane.
The Country School
The Golden Rule.
There would be your Brother, Pete, and an Apple
    Tree to Climb,
And a Day in the Kitchen, at your Mom's Side.
Or making a Snowman, a Night between Soft, Muslin
    Sheets,
And the Woodstove's Welcome Heat.

We can't Turn back the Clock on the Wall,
And there's no Crystal Ball, down the Hall.
So these, my Birthday Gifts to You will have To Do --
Replicas of Days Gone By, and My Best Wishes, Too.

These are the Things I would Give You for Your
    Birthday, if Only I Could.

THE CALL OF LONG AGO

I see Spinning Wheels, Washstands, Halltrees,
Old Ice Boxes, Buggies, and Me
In Rustling Petticoats and High Button Shoes
And Ladies of Fashion in Parasol and Plume.
I hear the Ring of the Blacksmith's Anvil
And in the Air is the Tallow - they're making Candles!
At the General Store there are Soft Muslins and Silks
from which to Choose,
And there goes a Peddler, in Handmade Leather Shoes.

I Love the Smell and the Look of the Wood.
Oak, Cherry or Pine, if it's Old, it's Good.
See that Grand, old Four-Poster Bed
Where, after their Labors, they Lay their Heads?
See the Butter Churn over there?
It catches my Eye and I Stare.
I see a Mother Kneading Dough for her Family's Bread,
And Men Toiling, building Homesteads.

Smell the Chicken Frying on the Old Cookstove,
And in the Fields Corn and Hay Grow.
I see Quilting Bees, Pig Roasts and the County Fair,
And Suntanned Children with Golden Hair.
When I look Up I see You
In your Sunday Best and your Highly Polished Boots.
I hear Horses Hooves on Bridges of Wooden Planks.
I see the old Country Church where they Gave Thanks,
Back when Everyone Knelt Together to Pray
And at Sunrise Greeted each New Day.

Had it not been for Circumstance
We might have Lived Then, Perchance.
When Time Stood Still -
By Wonder, Not By Will.

THE GREAT BIRD IN THE SKY

With the Rising Sun there could be seen a Circle of Smoke
    from the Teepee, as Evening Star Awoke.
She Arose from her Bed of Dried Rushes in the Dark,
    to the Distant Call of the Meadowlark.
She eagerly Slipped into a Fresh Tunic of Leather,
    and Stepped Outside to Survey the Weather.
She hungrily Ate the Mush made with Fresh Milk,
    and Smoothed her Long, Raven Hair of Silk.
She spent most of the Day with the Womenfolk Tanning
    Hides and grinding Corn,
While the Braves of the Tribe Carved their Slender Arrows
    and ornate Horns.
They Came Together for the Main Meal of the Day,
    then from the Camp she Decided to Slip Away.

She Tied her Horse to a Willow as she came upon a
    Clearing.
feasting on Berries, she Paused at the Sounds she was
    Hearing.
The View of the Fertile Valley Beyond
    revealed a Clear Stream that Beckoned her On.
She Swam and Bathed and Played in Her Reflection,
    then Lay in the Warm Sun without Detection.
She Lay there and Watched the Birds in the Sky,
    wishing to Join them - if Only she Could Fly.
She picked a Flower for Her hair,
    as a Remembrance of her Visit there.
She collected Colored Pebbles and Bid Speed to the
    Moccasins on her Feet,
As she Vowed to Return there again, a New Day to Meet.

She Joined in the Dance to the Maker of Rain,
    then left to the Beat of Drums as they Played.
The Setting of the Sun told her the End of Day was Not Far,
    and Evening Star was Sleepy as she Bid

5

Goodnight to the Stars.
The Twinkling Lights always Reminded her of the Story of
    Nineteen Summers Ago
Of how her Father, the Chief, had Named her for the
    Stars Shining on her Birth Below.
It was with This Thought in Mind,
    that Sweet Sleep she was Soon to Find.

THE DREAM:

It is now 75 degrees in Bangor, Maine.
There will be More Later on the Miami Hurricane.
A World News Report will be at Noon.
Please Stay Tuned.

Jennifer's alarm clock Rang out the Time
    just as the Church Bells started to Chime.
This was the Day she had Long Awaited,
    counted the Days and Anticipated.

She Stretched lazily between the Satin Sheets,
    Stretched, Yawned and Wiggled her Feet.
She Shampooed and Pampered and Pulled Out the Hot
    Rollers;
 Her Raven Hair of Silk Fell Gently over her Shoulders.

Ms. Jennifer Stone ate her Milk and Cereal,
    then Dressed in her Designer Suit and Snakeskin Heels.
She was the Prettiest Girl that you Could Hope to See;
    there was Indian Ancestry in her Family Tree.

The Taxi Cab through the Rush Hour Traffic did Arrive
    at International Airport for Flight 705.
She carefully Adjusted her Wide-Brimmed Hat;
    across the Aisle there was a French Diplomat.

The great Aircraft like a Shiny, Silver Bird,
    raced through the clouds Without Being Heard.

The Eiffel Tower was Approaching in Full View;
   she would Soon be Choosing a Souvenir, or Two.

Her Father was the Governor of One of the Fifty States;
   at Nineteen she was His Dedicated Associate.
All of her Time she Devoted
   and his Ambitions Faithfully Promoted.

How she had Needed some Rest and Relaxation,
   and had looked Forward to this Special Vacation.
What she wanted Most was to Find some Time
   to Gather her Thoughts and Restore her Peace of Mind.

Her Thoughts often Returned to Her Heritage of Long Ago.
Great Grandmother and her Father, the Chief, she would
   Love to Know.
Back then One Wouldn't have to Take a Trip,
   for nature was Waiting at their Fingertips.

She had Visions of Lying on the Beach
   where she Couldn't be Seen or Reached.
After Dinner she Danced by Moonlight as the Band Played,
   and made a Wish on a Bright Star that She could Stay.

The Next Morning her Mother's Voice drew her from the
   Deep Sleep in which she Lay,
As Evening Star Spoke of the Strange Trip into Another
   Time she had Made.
She Crept Outside and Eagerly Searched the Sky
   for the Return of The Great Bird she had seen Fly.

THERE'S GOING TO BE A SQUARE DANCE TONIGHT!

Open the Door,
Clear the Floor.....
There's going to be a Square Dance Tonight!

There's the Fiddler Man,
Let me Shake your Hand.....
Everyone's going to have a Good time Tonight!

Circle Skirts and your Best Blue Jeans,
If you Don't Know How, you Will when you Leave.....
Allemande Left and Do-si-do,
Swing your Partner, Here we Go!

Jon's Girl has the Long Brown Hair;
That's Mine, over There.....
Girls, Kick Off your Shoes, if you Want To,
And Everybody Shake the Blues!

Bow to Your Partner, Bow to Your Corner,
Bow to your Partners, One and All.
Promenade Around the Hall!

Birds in the Cage, Crow Flies In,
Dig for the Oyster, Dive Right In.
Bow to your Partner, Bow to your Corner.
Bow to your Partners, One and All,
And Take your Partner Home.

WAR AND PEACE

Wars and Rumors of War.
Man has Gone too Far.
Why does War Exist;
Why do Nations Resist
And Not Struggle for Peace?
Why is Peace Not a Fundamental Belief?

Chapter 2

Day-by-Day, a Reflection
Collection

(Volume 1 – Optimistic)

A G E

What 'Age' do I think I am, you Say?
Well, I Feel about 18, as of Today!
Not a Day Older, my outlook is Bright
As we Welcome the New Year in Tonight!

What is 'Age'?
It is Merely the 'Stage'
On which the Props of Life have been Set,
To Play Out our Parts, as 'Age' we Tend to Forget.

Like a good Book, my Cover is a Little Worn
And Inside the Pages number more than a Few.
Given Time, the Date you were Born
Will Fade in your Memory, too.

Suspended in Time
Two Minds Intertwine.
Let's Remain Ageless - Beginning Tonight.

DREAMS

Dreams,
Schemes.

Secret Longings of the Imagination,
Needing little more to Reach their Destination.....

Than a Penny 'Wishing Well'
And a Dream to Sell.

Paint a Picture in your Mind;
Turn Forward the Hands of Time.

Before your very Eyes will be a Parade
Of your Hopes and Dreams on Display.

ONLY A YEAR

If you had but a Year to Live,
What would you Give
In Exchange
For another Day?

How Great a Price to Pay
To live One More Day?
In your Depression
You know Some have Less.

In your Solitude, you Realize
Your Work in this World is Not Ready to Die.
It may Soon be Nearing it's Diminish,
But it is Not Nearly Finished.

You have Not Solved the Problems you Inherited,
And you are Arriving at your Goal Empty-Handed.
You have not Accomplished the Task set before You,
And your Journey will be Abruptly through.

Let us Allow ourselves to View Death as an Extension
Of Life, only in a New Dimension.
Let us Live our Lives in such a Way
That we may Approach that Coming Day
With Optimism and Receive
It, without being Deceived.

SEE THE OLD HOUSE?

See the Old House, in the Field, still Standing There?
   It's showing Signs of Wear,
And looks Smaller Now than it did Back Then.
Well, I can well Remember When
There was a Playhouse out Back
And Wood Piled up in a Stack.
And the Love was There.

A little Blond-Haired Girl with Delightful Ways
Played many Long and Happy Hours Away.
There were little White Ducks made out of Wood,
And her Boston Bulldog Understood
Her Mistress when she would Say,
"Please Sit Up for Me Today."
And the Love was There.

She Wore Sunbonnets and Starched Pinafores
Of Organdy, down by the Sycamore,
That her Mama Handmade.
Down there in the Shade.
Her Mama Planted Pretty Flowers
And they spent Many Happy Hours
Reading Little Stories
By the Morning Glories.
And the Love was There.

I Wonder if we could Step Inside?
Oh Yes, the Door is Open Wide.
See that Corner over There?
I used to Sit there in my Rocking Chair
That old Grampa 'A' made for me while I Learned
   my ABC's,
With my Old Doll that Played Make-Believe.
And the Love was There.
And the Sun came Out to Play.

Let's take a Walk on Down the Lane
To Gramma and Grampa 'G's house and back
    Again.
I Loved Her and her Cornbread and Buttermilk,
In her Fresh Apron, Pulling Cornsilks.
Mama and I would go to the Woods to dig
    Wildflowers,
Early in the Day, Before the Showers.
And the Love was There.
And the Sun Came Out to Play.

There's Daddy's Workshop of which I Never Tired,
Bringing him his Hammer and Pliers.
And when He would have some Pop,
He would Fill my Little Glass to the Top.
I Remember Linda Sue and Kenny down the Road,
And the Day I Stepped on a Toad.
And the Wasp Nest, way up High;
Mama got it Down, while I Spied.
We had a Black 'Model A' with a Big, Loud Horn;
We would Honk at a Lady in her Yard each 'Morn.
And the Love was There.
And the Sun Came Out to Play.

Her Daddy had to Leave Town to Look for Work
And With Him his Family Took.
Eventually they Moved Away,
And for Old Grampa 'A' it was a Sad Day,
For He Wore a Long Face
And Nothing his Frown Could Replace.
And the Love was There,
And the Rains Fell Down as if to Stay.

Old Grampa 'A' wrote Poems for his Brown-Eyed
    Miss, and he would Go
To the Mailbox every day, he Missed her So.

Let's Drive by Old Gramp's house, in Town.
There it is, with Memories All Around!
There's the Old Porch Swing.
Lightning Bugs I would Bring
To Gramma 'A' in a Jar.
"Now Honey, don't go too Far."
The Big Old Church, Rides in the Park,
Feeding the Birds, I think I'll Start
To walk around Back; what was that I Heard?
Looks like Sammy Squirrel chasing a Bird.
Grampa Loved Birds.
And the Love was There.

Walls Don't Talk,
And I Can't Walk
Back into Yesterday.
Only my Memories Remain
To remind me of the Past.
I have Come Home at Last.
And the Love was There.

SEVENTEEN WINTERS AGO

Seventeen Winters Ago I had a Wish, a Dream.
I had Waited so Long, it Seemed.

To be a Mother was my One Request,
And then, One Day, my Life was Blessed.

I knew not what Treasures Lay in Store
From this Small Bundle who would Grow, and
    More.....

It's been Even More than I had Hoped it would Be,
And You have made it a Reality.

SURVIVAL

Well, the "Big 30" has Arrived at Last!
My, how Time has Slipped through the "Corporate"
    Hourglass!
Your Sunshine and Perseverance has Inspired Us,
    One and All;
You've Survived, and you're Walking Tall!

You've Trucked in through Rain, Sleet and Cold;
Serving was your One and Only Goal.
You've come in Early and you've Stayed Late,
And you Didn't Charge for the Extra Freight.

Through "Stacks and Stacks of Letters"
You've Sifted over the Years;
Wouldn't you just Love a Nickel for each
Statistical Report and Unshed Tear?

Your old Relic of a Typewriter was a Longstanding
    Joke,
And the Duplicating Machine is Constantly Broke.
The guys Can't Spell or Write; well, their 6's look
    like b's;
But you seem to Sail Through with a certain Flair
    and Ease.

Your exceptional Ability to Align and Punctuate
Is Rivaled only by your Skill in Assuring your
    Boss is Never Late!
Yes, you "Deliver" with your own Style and Grace,
And Nary a Frown has Crossed your Face.

And what of the Meetings - Cancelled and
    Rescheduled, and the Incessant Phones Ringing?
Well, it's No Wonder at 4:30 we Notice it's a Little
    Song you're Singing!

It's definitely a Fact that you Deserve a Medal;
We've no Idea what would Suit you Better.
Hark! Is that your Boss we hear Calling?
"......won't you Drop what you're Doing and Type
    this Letter?"

Winner of:
Secretary's Week Contest, 1982
WAAM Radio
Ann Arbor, Michigan

THE PASSAGE OF TIME

I've Felt all along, Love of Mine,
That, just as Surely as the Passage of Time,
Someday you would make Known your Desire to Be
Self-Respecting and Always Free.

Just Remember, I've always Believed in You
And all you ever Planned to do,
It's just that Other Things stood in the Way
That you wanted to Try, Yesterday.

Today is the Day of Decision,
To decide which Life Goals need Revision.
It is something you must Do for Yourself.
You must Choose which things to Put on the Shelf.

Perhaps Now the Timing is Right,
Even as I Pray for you this Night.

Since I'm not There to help you Find your Way,
We must Rely on what Each Other has to Say.
So find yourself a Comfortable Chair;
I have some Thoughts I'd like to Share.....

***

You have already Earned an important Degree,
I'm sure you will readily Agree.
From Experience, the Great Teacher, comes
     Knowledge,
The School of Hard Knocks, the College.

So your Mistakes may not have been in Vain,
Vow you will Never Repeat them Again.
Put them in the Past and Reflect;
Gain all the Wisdom you can Collect.

Now, having Layed the Foundation,
Make the Most of this new-found Education.
Arrange your Life in such a way that you will Find
Some Bright Tomorrow will Truly be the Fulfillment
of "The Passage of Time."

THE SEASONS OF OUR LIVES

I remember Autumn and Shuffling through Leaves,
    the Rustle of Scarlet and Gold, formerly Green.....
How we would play Hide and Seek, and from Piles of
    Leaves we would Peek.

I remember Rolling Hills of Sparkling Snow;
    up the Cable Cars in Winter we would Go
To a Destination way up High,
    to our Location in the Sky.

I remember the World so Alive and Refreshed
    when Spring would take our Breath
Away with Birds Singing in Rhapsody,
    and the Earth new Life Bringing.

I remember Blue Skies
    and radiant Blue Eyes,
When you held me Close
    and we made a Toast
To Us,
Just Us.
It was on a Summer Starlit Night.
That was Before I Lost my Sight.

Now the World has taken on a Different Hue
    and every Sound and Scent is Reintroduced by You.
And you Spur me On
to the vast New World Beyond.

I Hear the Leaves Rustling beneath our Feet
    and Feel the Touch of your Hand as we Meet
The Seasons of our Lives,
    together, You and I.

YOU'RE A STAR

You're like a Many Faceted Diamond, so Fine....
Like a Single, Shining Star of the Night.

May your Radiance ever Shine,
And May your Star be ever Bright....

May you Always go Far,
But Never Out of Sight!

Chapter 3

Day-by-Day, a Reflection
Collection
(Volume 2 - Humorous)

ALL IN A DAY'S WORK

It's 5:00 o'clock, Time to Get Up and Turn Up the
    Heat,
And Fall Back into Bed for a Few Minutes more
    Sleep.
Oh No, the News report Woke me Up!
Now Where did I Put my Coffee Cup?
OK, you can Have a 10-Minute Stretch.
Yes, there's School Today, I'll 'Betcha!

Remember, the Hot Water is in Short Supply.
I get a Shower too, Don't I?
I Really should Wash a Load of Clothes.
Gosh, there's a Run in my Pantyhose!
Come on, Get Out of the Bathroom.
Either get Out, or I'm going to go 'Boom'!

What's for Breakfast, What have we got?
Same as Yesterday, *Thanks a Lot.*
Scrambled eggs, French Toast; Do you Want your
    Juice fresh-squeezed?
*Oh Mom, Can we have 'Silver Dollar Pancakes',
    please?*
Please Help me Put the Things Away.
I think I need a little Help today.

Did you Make your Bed?
Are you Listening to what I Said?
Did you Get your Teeth Brushed?
Why are We Always in such a Rush?
Did you Give the Dog her Medication?
Oh, Dear Lord, I think I Need a Vacation!

I Can't, I Have to Wash Dishes.
Oh, if only 'Dishes' were 'Wishes'!

I Can't, I'm on the Phone.
You Do it, Please, This time, Alone?
Oh, I'm so Excited, I'm Going to be an Aunt!
I Wonder, Did I Water the Plants?

Take out the Trash, Feed the Cats, wasn't there
Something Else to Do?
No, I'm Sorry, please Hurry, I haven't seen your Left
    Shoe.
No, we don't have Time to Play Basketball.
Son, you Sure are Getting Tall.
My Hair didn't Turn out Right.
Oh, I Forgot to Turn out the Lights.

I'll Pick you up at 5:00; Please, don't be Late, Alas!
I almost Forgot, Tonight's my Exercise Class!
Give me 'Kissy Bye',
Tell your Teacher I said Hi.
This time I'll Drop you Off at the School.
Now Remember 'The Golden Rule'.

I'm Running Late, No Place to Park.
I was Behind the School Bus at Main Street and
    Clark.
Yes, you'll have Your Report by Noon.
I'll Transcribe my Shorthand very Soon.
Two Different Meetings were Set for Ten O'Clock?
Yes, I'll Tell Him. It Shouldn't come as a Shock.

I must Leave Early, the Dentist is at Three.
What a Busy Day this is Going to Be.
The Mail is in a Stack.
It's just Time that I Lack!
I'd better Work through Lunch.
It's going to be a Busy Day, I've got a Hunch.

It's almost 5:00, I don't want to be Late.
I must Pick up my 'First Mate'.
Hi, how was School Today?
You have Lots of Homework, did you Say?
You have Basketball Practice, too?
I Don't Know what we're Going to Do!

Let me Stop a Minute and Check the Mail and the
    6:00 News.
Just Three Bills and an Ad on a Caribbean Cruise!
Here's a Letter from Brother. He Quit his Job and
    he's on his Way Home.
Says he's Lonesome and No More will be Roam.
No, Ice Cream will Spoil your Dinner.
Let me Put on Something to Simmer.

I'll Skip my Exercise Class Tonight.
Oh, my Waistline is a Sight!
Give me a Hug, Mother Loves you So Much.
Now Run Along and Put Away your Games and
    Such.

What's this, a Note just for Me?
Do you Know how Much you Mean to Me?
*"Mom, I Love You, I Love You, I Love You so Well.
If I were a Nut, I would Give you My Shell!"*
I Can't Believe it, you Wrote it Yourself?
Here, Let me Help you put the Games on the Shelf!

DADDY, WHEN CAN I DRIVE?

Little Bobby was Only Two
When he Knew
That some Day
He would Drive Away.
"Daddy, when I get Big like You
I'm going to Drive the Car, too."
He had Loved to Ride in Cars since he was Born,
......As he Leaned Over and Honked the Horn!

Bobby was Sitting by his Door
One day when he was Only Four.
He had a certain Gleam in his Eye
And his Dad thought he saw a Little Smile.
Son, have you Seen my Car Keys
"No, I don't know Where they Could Be."
He could imagine the Engine Soaring,
......As he Leaned over on his Door, so Boring!

Bobby was going on Eight
But he did not Hesitate,
To take note that his Folks were Watching
     Television,
As he Proceeded to Back the Car Out with Precision.
They saw a moving Blue Object sail past the Window
Just about the time Bobby Tore up the Left Fender.
He tried to Fix it with his Wrench.
His Thirst for Cars was Not Quenched!

Bobby and his Interest in Cars Grew as Time Passed.
He would read Road Signs and Follow the Map
On all the Family Vacations,
And even when they Stopped at the Gas Stations
He busily Mingled among all the Parked Cars.
He knew Each One by Name, so far.

29

He pay No Mind to his Clothes, and all the Soil,
As he helped his Dad Change the Oil!

At Long Last that Special Day Arrived.
Dad was Teaching Bobby how to Drive.
Saturday Night was to be the Homecoming Dance;
Bobby was Excited, this was his First Romance!
He took a Class in Driver's Education,
And was Prepared for this Special Occasion.
"Be Careful", he heard his Parents say,
As he Honked the Horn and Backed Out of the
    Driveway.

'DOUBLE X' LEX

Memories of the 'Good Old Days' come to Mind, taking
*   me Back....*
When all a Boy wanted was his own Knife,
*   Fishing Pole and Knapsack.*

Many an Hour Passed on 'Double X ' Lex's Knee.
I was just a Little Guy then, maybe Two or Three.
Wooden Toys he Carved for me, with his Knife, from
    a Tree Limb;
Yep, we 'Whittled' Time Away....I can still see Scenes
    of Him.

I sat Transfixed, while Red Apple Peel Circles
    dropped to the Floor.
Fascinated, 'Double X ' Lex's Knife quickly Cut to
    the Core.
As my Appeal for my Own Knife started to Grow,
I Dreamed of being an Indian.....with Knife, Arrow
    and Bow.

I Remember the Day when 'Double X' Lex's Knife
    sawed us out of a Thicket,
And how he let me Cut a Flower for Mother, instead
    of Picking It.
With rapt Attention, I listened while 'Double X ' Lex
    told me Stories of Case and Parker,
Sitting around the Campfire, carving Spears for
    Hotdogs at Sunset, while it got Darker.

Yes, Memories take me Back, and within my Gaze,
I'm Transported back to the 'Good Old Days'.
Times were Simpler way back Then
You know, you Remember When.

GARAGE SALE FEVER

Look at all these Garage Sales in the Paper!
There's always Lots - they Don't Seem to Taper.
I'll Put them in Street Order
And you Come on Over.
We'll have us a Ball;
Won't Cost Much at All!

Here's the First One - Everything but the Kitchen Sink!
There's the Perfect Frame for TJ's Picture - I Think.
Look at this Vase I bought for a Dime.
What Luck! Talk about a Find!
I sure wanted that Clock you bought for a Dollar.
Didn't want to Make a Scene, so I Didn't Holler!
Look at this Table for only Fifty Cents!
It's in Good Shape - Maybe just a Little Bent.
Some Paint and this Old Bench will look just Fine.
Let's keep Looking, we've got Plenty of Time.

Let's stop for Lunch, I'm Beat.
Does that Ad say Free Coffee on Maple Street?
Look at this Footstool,
And all of these Tools!
Won't Jim be Secretly Pleased?
You know how he Loves to Tease!
He always says there's Something Wrong with All of It.
He goes On and On and has his Little Fit.
Wow, we've Already been to Seven.
I think I've Died and Gone to Heaven!

Harris Street? Two miles South and make a Right.
About the time the Old Mill runs out of Sight.
We're going to know this Town like the Back of your
        Hand.
Wait 'till I get home with all this; Jim will Understand.
See you Next Week, Won't we have us a Ball?
And it Won't Cost much at All!

LET'S GO OUT . . . . .
FOR DINNER TONIGHT!

I've got an Idea, let's Go Out for Dinner Tonight!
OK, OK, I just Thought you Might!
Well, if I Did, What would you Like to Eat?
Oh, a nice Steak couldn't be Beat!

What about you? *Oh, let's Don't Go to a Fancy Place.*
Just a Hamburger sounds good. Do you still Want that Steak?
No, I think Seafood - Crab Legs,
    Lobster, or Shrimp would be Nice.
Or maybe some Chinese food, like Chop Suey and
    Brown Rice.

Well, I would like something Italian - Spaghetti, Pizza
    or Such.
And, of course, I like Souffle, Quiche, and Crepes just
    as Much.
And a nice Salad with lots of Veggies and Dressing
    would be Ideal.
The only thing, after I eat that, I couldn't hold my
    Meal!

What about Dessert? *What would you Like?*
Well, my First Choice would be Peach Parfait Delight.
And I always did like Hot Apple Pie a la Mode,
And Strawberry Triple-Dip Ice Cream Cones!

Oh my! Have you Looked at the Time?
By the time I get Dressed, it will be After Nine!
Let's just Stay Home and have a B-L-T.
Hey, that sounds Great to Me!

PAYDAY BLUES

It's Payday, it's Payday!
Let's you and I Celebrate!
Honey, you Deserve a Treat;
I'm Taking you Out to Eat!
Just a Minute before we Do,
I have some News for You.
Which do you want First, the Good or the Bad?
Let's Look at the Bills. Hey, don't Look so Sad.

Oh, I almost Forgot.
This phone bill's Hot.
And the House Payment is Due.
Oh yes, Jimmy's music lesson is, too.
What they Take for Taxes is a Sin.
With that, I could have mailed the Car Payment in.
If this Check goes around it will be an Achievement.
If it doesn't, I'll be in a State of Bereavement.

The Car needs Fixing up, it runs like a Wreck.
Maybe we better do That with the Next Check.
And I'm Tired of Mixing up Leftovers,
When I'm craving Benny's Turnovers.

***

You go Grocery Shopping and Keep the Change.
I'll Clean out the 'Frig and Rearrange Things.
Get something really Different this Time.
I don't care if you Spend every Dime.
Let's sit down and Talk about Setting
Up a Budget. This is all Getting
Us Nowhere fast. Let's set Aside for Beth's Education,
And how about taking that "Dreamed Of" Family Vacation?

You know, we've sure been Through some Stormy Weather,
But seems like we've really done A Lot Together.
Honey, here's the Good News!
No more will I Cry the Blues.
I'm just glad we've got it to Spend,
And make the "Rounds" Again!

THAT HORSE WILL WIN SOMEDAY!

"Wish I had some Extra Cash Tonight,
To Put on That Horse. That's Right!
That Horse is Going to Win, Some Day!"
Oh, that's what you Always Say.

"This one's Different, he's Going to Do Good.
Now, let me Make Myself Understood.
The Weather's Fine, the Horse Feels Great --
He's Moving Up! Appreciate!"

*"You Watch, he's a Born Champion, I Know.
And Someday I'll Say — I Told You So!"*

YOUR CHARMING RABBIT HAT

You Look so Elegant
In your Charming Rabbit Hat.
You look so Chic!
May I Entreat
You to Divulge your Source.
I Wouldn't Tell......of Course.....

Why thank you, thank you, how Kind.
No, I surely wouldn't Mind.
It came from Braskey's.
Thank you for Asking.
Oh, you look so Good in It,
And it's such a Nice Fit!

Did the Hat and Coat come as a Set?
No, it was a Streak of Luck, I Guess!
Would you like to Hear
How I came to have them, Dear?
As I was Waiting to Purchase the Coat,
I turned to the Lady Beside me and Spoke.
She herself was Dressed in Mink,
And it really made me Think.
I told her I almost felt Guilty,
And she looked at me Understandingly.
And, looking at the Coat.....
She replied, "Don't!"

Chapter 4

The Friendship Flower
Collection

CHAR 'S LEGACY

Char! Oh, there were so many, many, Fine Facets of
    'You'!
A Kaleidoscope of Colors, from Dazzling Emerald to
    Golden Violet-Blue!

Like a Gentle, Warm Breeze, on the Shores of an
    otherwise Ordinary Day,
You 'Blew In' to see Grandma Bea, or Us, and
    Always Knew just what to Do or Say.

We Feel that the Tug at our Aching Hearts will Never
    End, through Tears,
For what can Replace the Love of this Friend, or one
    so Dear?

***

You were an Energy Source, Bolting through the
    Azure Blue;
A Tidal Strength at Aerobics, with a Turquoise
    Ocean Hue.

The Worlds you Conquered were Complex and
    Numerous.....
With Excellence you Mastered.....Shorthand,
    Hungarian and Computers.

With the Warmth and Compassion of a Saint, for the
    Soup Kitchen and Orphan Home,
Your Healing Balm was Liberally Applied to those
    who Wait, and They were Not Alone.

There was Always 'Life' when you were Around,
Whether Silvery Serious, or the Sparkling Pink Clown.

Your Furry Friends Lapped up your Love, with
    Grateful Affection.
We can Close our Eyes and still See You, as if in a
    Reflection.

As a Wife, your Love will Forever Burn as a Purple
    Flame;
Never Flickering or Wavering, in Torrents your Love
    Came.

You Loved and Served the Great God of the
    Heavens.
God Adored You, as if Adding to the Bread, the
    Leaven.

Your Matchless Beauty knew No Rivals and was
    More than Skin Deep;
Reaching to the Depths of your Soul, we Harbour it
    in our Memories to Keep.

We can See You now, as if through a Shimmering
    Mist,
Carrying an Armful of Dewy Daisies, Sun-Kissed.

Let us One and All Live our Lives to Perpetuate
    'Char's Legacy',
So we, too, may Live in that Bright City, Eternally.

COFFEE KLATCH

"It's Good to Get Together for Coffee, Again.
We Haven't Done This since I Don't Know When!
What's been 'Going On'........it's already May;
What's Everybody Doing for Fun these Days?"
Well.....Steve still Sees his Old Girlfriend, Elaine, for
    Lunch, Two Times a Week.
It Seems they have a Lot of Things 'about which to
    Speak'.
You remember Donna, that he Dated Before her?
Well, she's Marrying Ken on the Twenty-Third.
Get this, he Hasn't even Received an Invitation
And he's taking Elaine to the Celebration!
Steve and Donna still Work for the Same Firm,
And she Drops Work Off for him at his Home, this
    Term.

"Does that Bother you, Yet?"
No, they're all Just Friends. *"I Bet."*
He's real Good Friends with Donna's Husband-to-Be.
They Bowl on Tuesday's down at 'Mister D's.'
This other Old, Old, Girlfriend, Marie, made him a
    Macrame and Dropped it By.
He still Takes her to Sunday Brunch, 'just to Say Hi'.
"Doesn't that bother you?" No, they're Just Friends.
"Well, you Never Know where it Might End.
What does he do?" He's in Sales - he can make
    Anything Sell.
"Looks like to me he has the Same Effect on Women, as
    Well!"
When he Decides they're not what he Wants to Marry,
He Moves on to the Next; he Doesn't Tarry.
"What Does this Guy Look Like, Anyway?"
Oh, You'll have to Meet him Some Day!
Here, he had his Picture Taken with his Daughters, just
    the Other Day.

*"Looks like Somebody had Three Girls and a Boy, I'd
    Say."*

"Kids, please Play Outdoors.
Come on, Tell me Some More."
No, <u>You</u> tell <u>Me</u> what's Going On!
Are you still Seeing Tom?

"Unfortunately No, he Must Be Seeing Two Other Girls.
His Life was <u>Always</u> in such a Whirl!"
How do you Know? *"Oh, I Sneaked a Peek.*
*There were Two Strange Cars in his Driveway just this
    Week."*
Mommy, Jon's making Faces at Me.

"Every Time we Meet,
My Heart still Skips a Beat."
Are you Concerned?
"No, Because I've Learned.
First of All, he's Married to his Job.
*And he's having an Affair with his Racehorse, named
    'Heart Throb'.*
Besides, I Don't Think he would Seriously Consider
Any Woman, who didn't Fifty Grand a Year Deliver!"

I've been Wanting to Ask, by the Way,
What Kind of Make-Up do you have on Today?
"Just my Skin, This is It....
What you See is what you Get!
I Hate to Tell you This, but the Dog is Out of the Yard."
I Wonder if he would Sell, if I didn't Charge?
Do you want to Take my Yellow Jewelry home?
Now Remember, this is only a Friendly Loan.
What Kind of Shirt do you Have On? What does it Say?
"My Barn or Yours?" Well, I've got News for you,
    Babe;

Nobody is going to Take You to the Barn Dressed like
That!
You may as well Go Put On an Old Straw Hat!

I Chased the Dog all Over Anderson's Yard.
Just Look at this Coat; How Much will the Cleaner's
Charge?
*"By the way, I Turned down the Heat while you were
Out."*
Must be Why the House is So Cold, No Doubt.
"Sure Wish <u>Something Exciting</u> would Happen -
Anywhere - Even on the Bus!
That's what We Need; That's What's the Matter with
Us!"

"Kids, Take Off your Muddy Boots."

Did you Ever go Out with That Guy that Owned the
Hardware Store?
"No, I Heard he went Back with his Wife, Forevermore."
How about the One they called Slim?
"Oh No, I Can't <u>Stand</u> Him!"

MY FAVORITE MAN

Our Daddy Loves Us, this we Know.
Oh Yes, there were Times when he said "No".
A Kinder, more Gentle Man you'll Never Find,
Even when he Bade us Mind.
He Dearly loves TJ and Jon, Kris, You and Me;
I only Wish I was 'Half as Good' as He.

He's Right There when you Need a Friend.
I've even seen him Help a Stranger, Time and Again.
He's a Walking Saint on Earth; only drinks Cokes,
Says no bad words, and makes lots of Funny, clean
    Jokes.
He has a Code of Honor on which he Stands,
He Tries to do Right by Every Man.
He Loves Life and Life's Simple Pleasures,
The Song of the Organ, Calliope and Train he
    Treasures.
He's so "Young at Heart", like a little Kid with a
    Toy!
Don't you Know he was a Darling little Boy?

He's a Strong man and when things get Tough,
Like old Pap-Pa, he's made of Strong Stuff.
He's a Strong man, he Doesn't Give Up;
He's a Fighter, when Life Gets Tough.
He's a Strong man, Determined, with Goals and
    Dreams.
Is it any Wonder we're as Proud as can Be?

Memories Linger as Time Surrenders,
And Never Dim the Thoughts, so Tender.
Other Men's Love through our Lives has Passed,
While Only our Dad's Love will Forever Last.
He makes us So Proud, I'm so glad he's Our Dad,
That's our "Pop", and he's My Favorite Man!

MY GOLF MAN

My Golf Man - sure Hope you're having a Ball!
May all your Strokes be Under Par - well, Almost All.

Hope Myrtle Beach suits you Guys to a Tee,
And 'Lots of Luck' on whatever Turf you May Be.

Now Don't go Overboard and Hit the Ball too Hard.
What if you Lost it in Someone's Backyard?

***

Just Remember, when the Lure of the Green is
Nearing an End,
There might be some 'Slopes' right Here you'd be
Interested in!

I'll Seal this little Rhyme with a Kiss,
To let you Know you are surely Missed.

I'll be Waiting where I've Always Been;
Can't wait 'till you're Back Home with me Again.

MY MOTHER, THE LADY

It is only Appropriate to Expound, as I make this
    Dedication,
With Words Profound to "The Lady" who has been
    My Consolation.
My Words, no doubt, will be Inadequate;
None seem to be quite Appropriate.
For She is Beyond Compare,
There is so much Beauty There.

The Intent of these Words is to be a Reflection,
Barring the Human Element, of Her unique
    Perfection.
She has been With Me through Thick and Thin,
Through Life's Problems. When will they End?
She is My Guardian Angel, sent from Above,
To Watch over Me in Peace and Love.
She helped me Learn Right from Wrong,
And helped me Become part of the World to which I
    Belong.

She saw to it that I received the Best Education,
And was my constant Motivation.
She Nurtured Me,
And Helped me to Feel Good about Me.
I wanted a Sister or Brother with all my Heart.
My Wish was granted; more Love her Heart could
    not Impart.
She doesn't Give to One without the Other,
Be it Houseslippers or a Pound of Butter.

She's a Consecrated Mother.

Through Times of Plenty she has Led.
In Times of Lean she has Fed.

She has been So Good to Me through the Years,
The mere Mention of it Brings Tears.
So, as I End this Poem for My Mother,
You must Know by Now, I Love Her as No Other.

MY PRECIOUS FRIEND

You're Like the Mirror in My Purse,
What I See There is Me in Reverse.
You are my Looking Glass, in You I See
Myself Reflected back, the Real Me.

When I'm Blue
So are You.
When I'm Not Glad,
You are Sad.

When Life is all Balloons and Pink Lemonade
And I'm Caught up in My Escapades,
We Talk and Laugh and Chatter Devour;
We're Surprised at the Time, for it's been Hours!

You Know my Idiosyncrasies
And You Still Like Me, for Me.
You Know and Like Me for What I am Within.
With all my Faults, on You I can Still Depend.

Knowing why I React as I do, in Certain Situations,
You Stand Up for me Without Hesitation.
When I Fail to find the Good in Others, and Life is
    an Empty Delusion,
You Help me see Another Side, Ending my
    Confusion.

You've Been There in My Darkest Hour, at the Altar
Of God, as I Stumble and Falter;
When I Can't see the Light that Daybreak Brings,
And my Eyes, with Tears Sting.

Just when I Think there is No One to Care,
I Turn Around and You are There.

This Tribute is Just for You, for You have Truly
    Been,
  My Precious Friend.

ONLY A FORTNIGHT AGO

Longingly, I Watched until he was Out of Sight. Taking
    Long Strides down Roosevelt's Hall,
Between classes, he Soared above the Rest with his
    Magic. Seems like Yesterday, after All.
I Gazed Intently at his Impassioned Plays on the
    Basketball Court, So
Dancelike, with Precisioned Frenzy---seems like Only a
    Fortnight Ago.

Roosevelt's going to Win, I Bet.
Up, Up, and Over, the Ball Sinks the Net!
Suddenly, the Whole School Body Rises in Unison and
    Rousing Cheer!
Wasn't that just Last Year?

Where did the Time Go, Where have We Been?
The Answers, "Everywhere" and "Nowhere", Sift
    through the Hourglass Together,
    Encompassed Within.
Why do I Ponder you Still, Deep within my Heart?
The Heart, where all Good Things have their Start.

He Wouldn't Know he was to Take a Part
Of this Fair Teenage Girl's Heart
To Far and Distant Places of the World,
While her World was Assorted Uphill Whirls and
    Downhill Swirls.

Now, a Lifetime Later, how Can this be Happening to
    Me?
I Turn to Take one Last Peek..... no Two..... no Three.
Can it be that I Saw him at the 40-Year Class Reunion,
    just Last Week?
A Week seems so Long Ago, now. Tell me, did he
    Really Kiss my Cheek?

THE FRIENDSHIP FLOWER

Relationships Come and Go,
While Friendships only Grow.
Relationships Tend to End,
While Nothing Lasts like a Friend.

A Friend will take Time to Listen and Time to Hear.
A Friend doesn't Last for Only a Year,
 or Two.
Friendships are like Flowers, once a Little Seed is
 Sown,
To Become a Colorful Bouquet, when Fully Grown.

Of course, when the Best of Both Worlds is Sought,
The Value is Beyond that of a Treasure Bought.

Whatever we Share,
May the Beauty found there
Endure through Joy and Tears.

Whatever we Share,
May nothing Interfere.
May it last for at least the Next Hundred Years.

THE LADY MANAGER

You're a Pleasure to Work with and to Know with your
    Kind and Gentle Ways.
Bringing quiet Dignity to the Office you Brighten all my
    Days.

You're a Leader in your Field --- "No Grass Grows"
    under your Feet,
And you put People at ease, both at Home and Overseas.

You're a Diplomat, making Suggestions here and There
    that will Impact the Company Image, showing that
    you Care.

You're always Quick to say 'Thank You' for even the
    Smallest favor Done,
And you take Time to Listen, showing Others they are
    Number One.

Your Faith in God speaks Volumes in this Fast-paced
    World
giving Balance to All Things when Life is in a Whirl.

May you go Far as you Move up the Corporate Ladder
    of Success.
Whatever you Do, wherever you Go,
I know you'll Always do Your Best!

THE MAN IN THE BROWN BUSINESS SUIT

The Man in the Brown Business Suit
Talks with Knowledge, is Polished and Fair.
Yet, as one Surveys the Profile of the Man,
There is still a decided Boyish Air.
He's Climbed the 'Ladder of Success',
And is Without any Hesitation or Ambiguity.
He's a Man of Distinction in his Field;
Yes, He's Reached his Full Maturity.

The Door is Always Open of the Man in the Brown
    Business Suit,
Giving Counsel to those in Need.
His Lifestyle reflects Generosity and Thoughtfulness,
Showing that he Cares, in Word and Deed.

His Love of the Water goes Back to his Younger
    Days,
On the Soft, Sandy Beaches of the Jersey Shore.
It was there, through Lifeguarding, Fishing, and
    Boating, he Played out his Dreams;
And where Fond Scenes will Dance of Aunt Faith,
    Forevermore.

With Camera in Hand, he Enjoys the Beauty of a
    Summer Day.
He has Respect for his Fellow Man, and All
    Creatures Great and Small;
He Leaves the Animals at Peace in their Lush, Green
    World.
He Believes in Tomorrow, and Loves God, Above All.
He found the Love of his Life,
His 'Dream Come True', his 'Lady Fair'.
Traveling all over the World,
He Takes her Everywhere.

From the Eastern Seaboard to California's Gold
Coast,
The Man has Left his Mark.
Still, this Man of Accomplishment is Humble and
Down-to-Earth,
And his Greatest Imprint is on his Family's and
Friend's Hearts.

Chapter 5

Superior Force
Collection

DREAM DYNASTYLAND

I've been Thinking about what you Said.
Seems you Need to Talk awhile Instead
Of keeping your Need for Motivation inside Yourself,
And possibly putting Personal Growth "on the Shelf".

As I stepped into this Starlit Night
I realized we are so Alike.
Every day can be such a Chore;
Even more than the Day Before.
Do you ever feel just like "Crawling back in the Sack",
Turning over, without even Looking Back?

That's how I felt until I Dreamed,
And in the Dream it Suddenly Seemed
That I was Alive.....and Refreshed!
All my Energies Meshed
Into a Singleness of Fruition,
A Single Spirit of Ambition.

For in my "Dream Dynastyland"
There was not One Idle Hand.
Not one Mind was Wasted
And each One Tasted
The Sweetness of Success and Fulfillment,
Happiness and Contentment.

I've decided I want to do My Part,
And by Example show those Close to my Heart,
My little Nieces and their Little Friends,
That we must Work Together and Send
Out the Message to the Next Generation.....
So they, too, may Make Preparation.

58

TAKE 2 MINUTES

Just Take 2 Minutes each Day
To Read and Hear what I have to Say.
There IS Hope in your Life, Today.
And Yes, it was Always that Way.

You are Strong.
It's Not that you can do no Wrong,
But you are Literally a Tower of Strength.

Help my Friend.....this day to Only make Plans,
Not to Plan the Outcome of her Expectations.
She is the Outcome of the Master Hand.
Her Superior Force is the Supreme Celebration.

Help my Friend.....this day to be All she can Be;
Self--Confident in her Ability
And Help her to Help Others to See
What she Sees now through Humility.

Help my Friend.....from the Trials of Life to be Freely
    Detached,
So to the Will of God she may be Firmly Attached.
Help her to Rid herself of Rudeness and
    Resentments,
To replace them with Sincerity and Sentiments.

Help my Friend.....to Achieve Contentment
Through the Above,
Her Serenity and Fulfillment
Of Peace and Love.

Thank You for taking 2 Minutes Today
To Hear what I had to Say.
There IS Hope in your Life Today.
Oh Yes, and it's Here to Stay!

59

THE PASSAGE OF TIME

I've Felt all along, Love of Mine,
That, just as Surely as the Passage of Time,
Someday you would make Known your Desire to Be
Self-Respecting and Always Free.

Just Remember, I've always Believed in You
And all you ever Planned to do,
It's just that Other Things stood in the Way
That you wanted to Try, Yesterday.

Today is the Day of Decision,
To decide which Life Goals need Revision.
It is something you must Do for Yourself.
You must Choose which things to Put on the Shelf.

Perhaps Now the Timing is Right,
Even as I Pray for you this Night.

Since I'm not There to help you Find your Way,
We must Rely on what Each Other has to Say.
So find yourself a Comfortable Chair;
I have some Thoughts I'd like to Share.....

You have already Earned an important Degree,
I'm sure you will readily Agree.
From Experience, the Great Teacher, comes
*   Knowledge,*
The School of Hard Knocks, the College.

So your Mistakes may not have been in Vain,
Vow you will Never Repeat them Again.
Put them in the Past and Reflect;
Gain all the Wisdom you can Collect.

Now, having Layed the Foundation,
Make the Most of this new-found Education.
Arrange your Life in such a way that you will Find
Some Bright Tomorrow will Truly be the Fulfillment of
    "The Passage of Time."

TIME IN

You have "One Year" Sobriety, I Overheard you
    Say?
That's Quite a While. Seems you've Stayed
True to your Purpose for a Long Time.
A Year is a Milestone in Men's Minds.

A Marker in the Sands of Time.
A Ministry says the Clock that Chimes.
A Foothold in a Raging River
That only "Time In" can Deliver.

Be it 6 Months or 30 Years, Every Day is Your
    Anniversary,
And there's No Competition - for the World Record
    for Conquering Adversity
Is the one felt Deep within your Own Heart --
Knowing *this time* you've Really got Your "Start".

Chapter 6

On the Way to.....
The Treestump Tea Party
Collection

A HAPPY YESTERDAY

My Little One, it's hard for Me,
All by Myself, Alone to Be
Your Father, Mother, Sister and Brother.
For I am Only One. I am just your Mother.

I Try so hard to make you a Good Home,
And spend Lots of Time with you, Alone.
My Greatest Joy is being with You.
Do you Enjoy being with me, Too?

It's Upsetting when you don't Mind,
And so I Sometimes Take the Time
To Explain that it's for your Own Good.
If Only you Understood.

Is there Anything you could Give
So our Lives more Peaceful we could Live?
Think about it for a While.
I'm sure you can Think of Something, my Child.

And so, My Little One, please Know
That I Need you and Love you So.
Let us Live our Lives in such a Way
That each Tomorrow will be the Memory of.....
A Happy Yesterday.

HOBO, THE CROSS-EYED CAT

Hobo, Hobo, Where Are you At?
Now get Out of there, Scat!
I Missed your Greeting Today.
Meow-I! What Did you Say?
Meow-I! Meow-I!
Come, get your Dinner.
Seems you're Getting Thinner.
You're such a N-i-c-e Cat!
Hobo, Where are you At?

He's in the Clothesbasket, having a Good Time.
Watch out! I think he's Getting ready to Climb!
Now he's Under the Bed!
You Sure Do Like to be Fed.
Hobo's a Little Bit of a 'Cross-Eyed' Cat.
Doesn't Matter, though - he Can See where's he's At!
He's so Homely, he's Cute,
And he Owns Two Pair of Black Boots.
Look at that Tail go Back and Forth!
He Spied a Strange Cat on the Back Porch.
In his Luxurious, Satiny-Soft Fur,
I sometimes Forget - that He isn't a Her!

He's a King at Agility,
And has Exceptional Mentality.
Meow-I! Meow-I!
That's a Pretty Intelligent Conversation!
You're a Pretty Smart Cat, in My Estimation!

ON THE WAY TO......
THE TREESTUMP TEA PARTY

Hoorah! Hoorah!
Today's The Day!

Chattering, Corky Chipmunk, with much Delight
Scampered from his Haven into the Sunlight!
He Tumbled on the Forest Floor's warm, green Grass,
Doing Handsprings and Somersaults. At long Last.....
The Magical Day had Arrived!
He and his Friends were due at Five
To meet Miss Melanie for a Treestump Tea Party.
Now he must go Wake Up the Others, starting
With the Twins, Sally and Sammy Squirrel.
Oh, there they were in a Happy Whirl,
Gathering nuts for the Long, cold Winter ahead.
Very Soon they would be at the Party, instead!

This would be the Last Party of the Season,
And "Small Person", their Hostess, was the Reason,
Excitement, like Electricity, could be Felt in the Woods
        today.
All the Animals Adored their Little Friend who often
        Came to Play.
They all Knew the Party would Go By too Fast,
Leaving only Memories through the Winter's Blast.
The next 'Tea Party' would be an Event of Spring.
Each Furry Friend chose from his Habitat
A Gift for Melanie to Treasure and to Look At,
To remember Playful, Pleasant Scenes of the Past,
Until Spring, when they would be Together at Last.

Dixie, the Deer, was Basking by the Stream,
Nibbling on Berries as if in a Dream.

She Turned, then Sprang Eagerly to Join the Gang,
  Pausing briefly, Gathering her Gift as she Sang........

........A Happy Tune and her Small, Dancing Feet
Rushed Excitedly, the Others to Meet.
Melanie was the Delight of this Vast Animal Land,
Since she Set the Sparrow's Wing, with her own Small
      Hand,
And Touched with Love each Living Thing.
Dixie Recalled how Melanie would Sing
Soft Melodies when it was their Nap Time,
And her Favorite Tree that Melanie loved to Climb.

From Nuts, Sally and Sammy had Fashioned a
      Jumprope.
Together they Pulled it through the Woods with the One
      Hope
That Melanie would like their Present the Best!
Together they Tugged - what a True Test!
Corky had Shined a V-shaped Limb, for Melanie a new
      Slingshot -
How she Loved to Try for Apples - Whether she got One
      or Not!
In Dixie's Mouth was a Single, Wild Rose of White.
Watching it from a Bud, it had Bloomed in the Night.
For "Purity of Spirit" it had been Intended,
And for All the Small Hearts Melanie so Often had
      Mended.
What a Spectacular Sight, indeed, it was to See
The Animals as they Danced Along, so Merrily.

The Cubs, Ted and Tiger, and Lizzie the Lion,
Had Slipped away from the Zoo,
For they Each Loved Melanie and Wanted to be Part
of the Treestump Tea Party, too!
There was Roxanne Robin, Flying low Overhead,
While Timothy Turtle slowly Carried his Bed.

Rex, the Rabbit, and his Family were Bringing up the
   Rear.
There were Bon-Bon, Beth and Buford Bullfrog, too,
   trying to Steer
And Keep Everyone in a Neat, Straight Line.
My! Oh My! Were they Running Out of Time?
Just as they Neared the Clearing and the Treestump,
there Fluttered By.....
a Tiny, Perfect Leaf, which Turned to Gold and Lit up
   the Sky!
They Carried it Gingerly the Rest of the Journey,
for they Knew it surely was "Fate"! It was Meant to Be!

THE ALPHABET LOVE STORY

A   is for Apple, 'cause you're the "Apple of My Eye".

B   is for Baffle, you're so Full of Surprise.

C   is for Capable, you can Do Anything!

D   is for the Dandelions, you Bring to me in Spring.

E   is for the Ecstasy when I'm Held in your Embrace.

F   is for the Feeling that Sweeps over me as I Touch your Face.

G   is for your Gestures, your Gaze, One and All, and the Gladness you Give.

H   is for your Habits, your Hello when you Call, and for the Happiness Each Day we Live.

I   is for Industrious, Intelligent, too, and the Ideas Stemming from your Mind.

J   is for your Jokes, Jolly-You, and all our Journeys through Time.

K   is for the Know-how in things you do, and your Knee-deep thirst for Knowledge.

L   is for wanting Latitude, and the Love and Laughter you Lavish on me.

M   is for the Mountains High that we've Climbed Together.

N   is for when you're "Naughty-but-Nice", your Needs, and Newsman when you give the Weather.

O   is for your Oneness, how you Observe Others, and how you Occupy my Thoughts.

P   is for your Palette of Personality Colors, and the Piggy Bank you Bought.

Q   is for how you Qualify for all my Attention, your Quick Wit, and your Quietude.

R   is for the Races that we've Won, and for Other People's Rationale that you Pursue.

S   is for the Significance of Situations where we've been, your Scars, your Saunter and your favorite Shoes.

T   is for being "Tuned In", for your Tenderness and Togetherness in Things we Do.

U   is for being Unparalleled and Unbiased, and Unaffected by Attention.

V   is for being Vehement when you're Right, for Victories won, and your Virtues too Numerous to Mention.

W   is for Your Willpower, your Warmth and being Well-groomed,

X   is for being a "Xylophone" through the Hours, and the Chords you've Changed into Melodious Tunes.

Y   is for Yesteryear which has Slipped Away with your Youth.

Z   is for your Zest and Zip in Your Quest for Truth.

Chapter 7

In the Village Chapel
Collection

BELATED ROSES

I've Never Sent Flowers to a Man before,
But These are Long Overdue.
Please Say we can Begin Once More,
'Cause Darling, I do Love You.

For Angry Words Spoken in Haste,
And Other Things that Caused you Pain.
I can See it was All such a Waste,
Please let us Begin Again.

***

Your Love Came when I Needed it Most,
And No One Else can Take your Place.
Our Romance should have been a Happy Time;
If only Some Things could be Erased.

The White Rose is for the Love you've Shown,
Many Times, in Many Ways.
The Red Rose says I Can't Love Alone.
Please Tell me the Words I Long to
Hear you Say.

BLUE DAYS OF REGRET

After All This Time I still Find it Hard to Believe
That you're Not Really Here with Me.
I well Recall the Day
When you Went Away.
How you Deceived Me, right up to the End.
And Didn't even Value Me, as a Friend.
You Left Me Devastated, without Warning.
It was all so Humiliating and Alarming.
As I Loved you One More Time,
And Held On to what I Thought was Mine,
Little did I know it would be the Last.
I can Still see Your Face Pushed Up Against the
    Glass.

Seasons have Passed and I have Matured;
Time has Elapsed as I have Endured
The Pain,
The Strain.
Within Me Your Love Always Stays.
Thinking I See you, I Call Out Your Name.
I see a Truck with Running Lights,
And Watch Until it's Out of Sight;
The Chair where you Always Sat,
The Way you Wore your Western Hat;
A Face in the Crowd,
The Stature of a Man, so Proud.

Do you Ever Regret,
Have Blue Days Overtaken and Upset
You, in these Two Long Years;
Two Long Years of Tears?
A Part of Me
Will Always Be

Torn from Missing You,
From Not Having You,
And Yet Somehow I know Deep Inside
That you Miss me Tonight.

DAUGHTER OF MINE

Daughter of Mine, my Heart is Filled with Sorrow,
For you will Marry on the Morrow.
My Sorrow is for Myself, and as I Weep
I Know, because I Love You so, I do want
Your Life to be Complete,
as Mine Was.

I could Never Keep you from Knowing
The Joy that will be Yours in Showing
The World that You and He are as One,
For in Him I have Truly Found the Son
That I Never Had.

You will be a Dedicated Wife,
And you Deserve to have a Happy Life.
And in my Sadness I Realize
That Mothers down through Time Sympathize
With me Tonight.

So Come to me Once More, Daughter of Mine,
And Let me Hold you One More Time....
And Receive unto Myself a Part of Your Strength
You have Given to me so many Times, at Length,
Since you were but a Child.

Here, the Locket I now Wear is Yours.
Let me Put in on You, and Assure
You, that the Love found Inside
Was Given me as I was to Become a Bride.
It was on a Night like This
And is Sealed with Grandma's Kiss.
It Seems like Yesterday.

DREAMS I'M AFRAID TO SPEAK

I've been Afraid to Tell you
What I really Feel Inside,
For Fear of Losing what I
Thought I would Never Find.
More than Anything Else in this Life
I have Longed to be Your Wife;
To Work, Plan and Dream,
And Concoct Life's Favorite Schemes.
I Don't Wish to Own You, Merely to Share,
And to Know the Happiness to be Found There.

Must I Wait until 'Leap Year' is in Sight
When I would Then have the Right;
To Ask you what is Deep Within my Heart,
To Offer you That of which Only You could be a
    Part?
Would you Marry Me if I Asked?
Or does it Seem too Great a Task?
Do you Sometimes Find your Thoughts Returning
To Complete a Love within you Yearning?
If you Think there's a Chance
To Extend our Romance,
Then some day, Beyond the Bridge that Brought us
    Together,
Let us Meet and Know the Extent of Love Without
    Measure.

You know I would Follow you Anywhere;
It's True, I would Go without a Single Care.
I would Follow you at the 'Drop of a Hat '
Because for me, you are 'Where it's At '.
You Want it, Too.
I Know you Do.
I have Dreams I'm Afraid to Speak
And All I have I Lay at your Feet.

I Know we could Make It if we Wanted to Try,
And Ours wouldn't be the Kind that Money Buys.
I love you Better than Anything in this Life.
For you I would Endure Sorrow, Pain and Strife.
More than Anything Else in this Life
I have Longed to be Your Wife.

IN THE VILLAGE CHAPEL

She was Dressed in Pure White,
And by the Candlelight
No One saw the Tears, as She said "Yes",
That Fell down the Cheeks of All the Guests.

She was Everyone's Pride and Joy
As she Promised this mere Boy
To Love, Honor and Cherish
For Always, through their Marriage.

There was a Supreme Presence in the Village Chapel
　　that Day,
And it came to Join them and to Stay,
To Guide Her and the Lad.
No One need Look so Sad.

**

Their Love was Blessed from the Beginning.
With Love, there is No Ending.
Hosts of Angels Sang
As the Chapel Bells Rang.

That was Fifty Years ago.
I Chose to Return here So
As to Relive the Magic of That Day
When I Looked into Your Eyes and Heard you Say...

In Hushed Tones, your Wedding Vows to Me.
I Could Not Envision Adequately
The Future Role you were to Play Towards
Bringing Me Joy from That Day Forward.

**

As They Knelt to Pray
In the Village Chapel that Day
Hosts of Angels Sang
As the Chapel Bells Rang.
The Radiant Sun Shone In
And Blessed their Love Again.

JOHNNIE, CAN YOU HEAR ME?

Johnnie, can you hear me? This is Cindy speaking.

Pleasant Memories of Us came to mind Today,
Of when we were Children, together at Play.
Then, Overnight it seemed, we had grown Tall;
Left behind were Days of Toy Trucks and Dolls.

I can still see Scenes of you and I playing Football,
As the years turned Baseball Summers into Fall.
We grew up Together, then Somehow we Drifted
    Apart.
Now, Time has had it's Own Way of Relinking our
    Hearts.

On the River of Life, we each Drifted about in our
    Own Canoe,
Then one Magical Day I looked up and saw You!
And, as our Two Worlds merge as One, before God,
    Today,
I can only Gaze at You and Say......

In Sickness and In Health, I will Love you Afresh,
For my Feelings for You go Beyond Flesh.
'Til Death do us Part, I'll Love you through Pain and
    Strife.
My Fondest Dream is to be Your Wife.

I'll Need your Love until I Grow Old.
I'll Return it to You a Hundredfold!

Cindy and Johnnie, Can You Hear Me? This is God
    speaking.

My Children, Marriage is Honorable, designed by

My Own Hand.
Holy Matrimony is Ordained between a Woman and
a Man.
Your Vows will be Over in a Little While, it's True,
So, Store them in Your Hearts, to last a Lifetime
Through.

In the Bible is the Guideline for a Godly Home,
And, if followed, would Not Allow for Sin to Roam.
Nor will Family Values Decline
If People practice these Words Divine.

Follow the Roadmap to Heaven, found within it's
Pages.
Jesus died to be Mankind's Substitute, for Sin's
Wages.
Believe, and your Souls will Never have to Die,
And you can Live with Me some day in the Sky!

Make a Family Altar, I love it when you Pray.
And I Promise to be Here for you 24 Hours a Day.
More than the Love you Feel for Each Other,
you are to Love and Honor Me.
And my Blessings will Abide on your Home -
Faithfully!

I'll Need your Love until you Both grow Old.
I'll Return it to you Ten Thousand Fold!

LEAVE ME IF YOU NEED TO

Leave Me if you Need To,
I Do Understand.
Just Remember when you're in Texas,
You'll Still be My Man.
Yes, these are Tears you see Running down My
    Cheeks;
Leave Me if you Need To,
No Other Arms will I Seek.

Yes, I will be True;
You must Go Now and do what's Best for You.
I have Found the One I Sought;
To Look at Another would Only be for Naught.

Yes, I will be True,
And not just because you Asked me To.
It is Something I want for Myself;
I would Rather be Alone than with Someone Else.

MAN OF MY DREAMS

The Spark you Lit now Burns as a Flame,
If I Love You am I Really to Blame?
Though for a Time I only Admired you from Afar,
I Love You Now for All the Wonderful Things you
    Are.

A Rich Man in More Ways than I Can Count,
Blessed, your Virtues Spill Over the 'Fount.
You are Wisdom, Truth, and Knowledge,
And they Teach Honor at Your College.

Each day I Discover a New Reason to Look Up to
    You.
I Stand Back in Awe of All the Things you Can Do.
You are Industrious, with a Capital "I".
Not Wasting any Time, you Know How to Capitalize.

You, Sir, are Mr. Ambition.
You have Crossed this River and Won.
In all the Galaxy I Searched but Never Found
Your Equal; then you Gently Touched Down.

You are as Bright and Shining as the Sun.
"Superman", you're Still Going Strong when Day is
    Done.
As Big as the Moon, your Heart Overflows with
    Kindness.
Luckily, this Little Star doesn't have Night Blindness!

Your Jokes leave me Smiling all through the Day
And I Sneak a "Peek" as you Turn Away..
You're 'Layed Back' and Mellow and Don't Put on
    any Airs.
Not Lacking in Class, I must say, Sir, you Do have a
    Flair.

Your Eyes Light Up by Day and by Night.
Your Smile sends Shivers at the Sight.
You Don't Pretend, you're a Fighter and a Lover.
When the Storms of Life Descend, you Don't Run for
    Cover.

It's Time for you To Go and I Want You to Stay.
I Love the Look of You; you Take my Breath Away.
You are a Bearded Wonder, a Most Spectacular
    Sight.
When Touched by You I Feel the Thunder; you Are
    my Delight.

Man of Muscle, Hard as Iron and Strong as Steel,
When you Wrap your Arms Around Me it's
    Tenderness I Feel.
Through the Breeze of the Open Window I again
    Realize
I'm so Glad you are Mine Tonight.

Man of Purpose and Goals, and Man of My Dreams,
Did you Ever Think of 'You and Me' in Life's
    Mainstream?
You ask, will My Love last a Lifetime Through?
I only know I want to Share it with You.

I Hear the Echo of your Voice
Carefully Considering the Choice.
All I know is, I Love what I See
And we have All Eternity.

MY FONDEST DREAM

You Asked me what I Wanted,
Well, I've Known for Some Time, you See;
Listen as I Tell You
Just how I Want my Life to Be.

I can't Picture even One Day
When you would not be at the Start;
My Life now Revolves around You,
On this, the Day of Hearts.
(Alternate line: You are so Close to my Heart)

So Sweet and Gentle is your Love,
I'll make you Happy the Rest of My Life.
I Wish for the Chance to Show You;
My Fondest Dream is to be Your Wife.

Winner of Red Roses
Valentine's Day Poetry Contest, 1983
WAAM Radio
Ann Arbor, Michigan

85

ON BEYER'S OLD 4TH FLOOR
- That Magical Night -

It was just before Christmas, on Monday, December 21st,
1998.....

The rooms were Empty that day, on Beyer's Old 4th Floor.
Very soon Maternity would be moved.....to be Restored
At St. Joseph Hospital, an Expansion of their Ward.
This Move would be a Disruption for some---it would be
Hard
For those Beyer Nurses who had spent their Lives
Here, Bringing into the World "New Life".
For Years, the Town's Babies "First Moments" were
Sheltered Here,
Met with the loving Nurse's kind and gentle Care.

When I Awoke, I was told I was possibly the last patient on
Beyer's Maternity 4th Floor.
Realization hit me, this was the Floor where Jon & Susie
were born, 27 and 48 years Before!
In a Whirl, Memories flooded my Heart and Mind,
That Magical Night, And I felt Transported back into Time!

It was if an Angel of the Lord
Ushered me thru Beyer's old 4th Floor.
It was if an Angel of the Lord
Allowed me to Revisit the day You were Born!
It was if an Angel of the Lord took me by the Hand,
And Allowed me to Roam this Promised Land.

Tuesday Midnight, a Commotion was heard up and down
the Floor,
As an expectant Mother was Wheeled through the Door.
Now there were Two of us on Beyer's Old 4th Floor.....
when the Sound of New Life filled the Corridor!

And very soon we were Three,
the New Mom, her Baby and Me.
Or was it Four,
With the Angel of the Lord?

Beyer's Old 4th Floor was Filled with the Baby's strong
    Cries,
Soon to be Replaced with the crooning of Nurses singing
    soft Lullabies.
The place was Alive with Mirth and Gladness;
And the "Blue Bundle" had Added an Element of Holiness
That Magical Night, felt at the Heart's Core.....
Brought to Bless Beyer's Old 4th Floor!

And very soon we were Three, the New Mom, her Baby and
    Me.
Or was it Four,
With the Angel of the Lord?

OPPORTUNITY IS HER NAME

The Woman in Red.....

The Mood is Light
This Time of Night.
The Mood is Warm and Mellow
In Hearts of Girl and Fellow.

The Tinkling of the Melting Ice
Twinkles in their Meeting Eyes.
The Music slowly Surrounds Them
As their own Music Promises to Send
Them into a Sea of Delight.
On this Sensuous and Steamy Night.

Opportunity is Her Name.
Opportunity is Her Game.
Changing Partners, changing Scenes,
Fulfilling Man's most basic Need.

Although they Never met before Tonight,
Leaving Together they will Soon be Out of Sight.
He Longs to be Locked in a Lover's Embrace.
Very Soon they will be Alone, at Her Place.

He Plays her Body like an Instrument,
Until his Passion has been Spent.
The Conquest Over, he will be Content for a While,
Until Opportunity Appears again, with a Smile.

Although the Faces Change,
They are really One, the Same.
His Need to Love Repeats
In his Mind, it's Mission to Complete.

The Woman in Black.....

This way of Life seemed Fine in Theory.
One Problem — his Soul is Weary
For a Love that's Lasting.
He Feels as though his Soul is Fasting.

His Nights on the Town,
His Partying Around,
Finally Fail to Render a Deep Satisfaction
Based on mere Physical Attraction.

His Way of Life seemed Right in his Teens,
His Thirties, and In-Between.
By Forty it was Rare
To have a Meaningful Affair.

Experiences have Made him the Man he is Today.
If they were Wrong, I'm not the One to Say.
Experiences have Built the Man to a New Maturity.
Girls of His Past hold Less and Less Allure.

He needs a Woman that Cares.
One who can Also her Body Bare
And with it her Mind, and to him Assign
The Inner Happiness he Seeks to Find.

This Time the Partners won't Change,
And the Names will Stay the Same.
Fulfilling this Man's Deepest Need,
She will Complement him.....Totally.

THE ARMS THAT ONCE HELD ME

The Arms that once Held Me
Now want to be Free;
If we hadn't been so Close,
It wouldn't Matter to Me.

The Lips that Warmed me with their Touch
Now don't Seek mine as Much;
If we hadn't Been so Close,
I could Bear all Such.

The Man that Stirred me just Yesterday
Has Turned and Gone his Way;
Had we not been so Close,
I wouldn't Long for him to Stay.

We've made Resolutions
In the Hope of finding Solutions;
To help us Survive our Predicament
We've attempted Self-Improvement.

My Feelings for You
Unchanged, will Remain.
They Reach Above and Beyond
What we knew Yesterday.

Deprive me of Yourself
And I'll Love you Afresh,
For my Feelings for You
Go beyond Flesh.

The Arms that Once Held Me
Will Hold me Again.
I've Love enough to last;
I can Wait until Then.

THE LOW ROAD

We're Lost on an Endless Ocean,
Bereft of all Emotion.
We're Lost on a Sea of Despair.
Oh God, can't our Marriage please be Repaired?
The Tide and the Waves Sting my Face.
The Turbulent Waters are Relentless in their Chase.

All my Feelings behind my Heart's Door are Locked.
We must Stop now and take Stock.
How did things get in this Condition?
When did we Stop taking Time to Listen?
We thought we Knew each other so Well,
And now, only Time will Tell.

There's Nothing much left of our Happy Home,
And I'm going to be Left here all Alone.
We can't even Communicate.
We need to, before it's too Late.
No one Person is in the Wrong.
We're just not Singing the Same Song.

He just Left, with his things, out the Side Door.
He doesn't Love me Anymore.
You've Listened to me without Hesitation.
You seem to Understand my Situation.
You don't even Know my Name,
And I may Never Pass this way Again.

I Understand your Pain.
Some of my Scars still Remain.
I know, because I've been there Before;
When you Realize the Love isn't there Anymore.
I needed Someone just as you Do,
And was met with a Hearing Ear, Too.

Is there Some way I can Repay You?

Yes, by Someday putting yourself in Another's Shoes.
From the Frying Pan into the Fire, Beware.
People Turn and People Stare.
Determine to Exit the Low Road at the Lane of
Happiness,
And in Time you will Recall the Rough Spots Less and
Less.

THE RIVERS OF MY NEED

You Walked into My Life so Bold,
Your Presence Shook my very Soul.
You Lifted me Up from the Start;
Your Nearness Flooded my Heart.

Ever Since the Day you Took Residence in My Mind,
One Thought of You and I Find,
There's a Peace within Me Now.
You're the Reason, Yet you Dare to ask "How?"

No Other Man on Earth
Could Gift Me with this Rebirth.
Of all the Great Purchases in Recorded History,
More Precious than Gold was Your Gift to Me.

I Need You to Care
And to Always be There.
I'll Need Your Love until I Grow Old.
I'll Return it to You a Hundredfold.

How Can the Needs of this Woman be Measured,
When Just the Sound of Your Voice is so Richly
    Treasured?

How Can the Needs of this Woman be Met?
Without You they Can't, and Yet....
The Rivers of My Need are Without End,
Swiftly Flowing, for You they Send.

Do you Still Dare to Doubt,
When it is You I Need and Can't do Without?
No One Else could Take your Place.
It is a Fact that I have Faced.
Can you Understand why My Hopes and Plans
Are Wrapped up in You, My Marvelous Man?

93

Just to be Near You and to See
What Lies in Store for You and Me.
Do We Share these Feelings Rare,
Or were We not Meant to be a Pair?
Will We Climb the Stairway of Time as a Team?
Will We go Hand-in-Hand, or are We just a Dream?

THE STRANGER

I want a Man that's "Taken" with Me,
Not "Taken" with each Pretty Face he Sees.
I want a Man that's Totally Mine,
One that can Stand the Test of Time.
Every time I look Back, you're Looking Again;
Could it be a Trait Inherent in Man?

I Sense the Passion you Feel for "The Stranger";
It causes me to Retreat in Anger.
For a Moment I Long to be "The Stranger",
To Sense the Silent Messages meant only for Her.
For a Time I was truly "The Stranger",
Unaware of any Risk or Danger.

Fate has brought us to this Point in Time;
You Seek your Rainbow; I'll seek Mine.
There must be Someone Searching for Me,
Or does he Exist only in my Fantasy?

THE SUNSHINE SHIP

Some say Love is a Gift and it's Value Lost,
When it's not Shared - like Cake without the Frost.
Ponder with me for a Minute.....
The World, with No Love in it.

Imagine Love as an Island far out in the Sea,
Transient, Inaccessible, Wild and Free.
I know, for you and I Sailed there, in my Dreams.
And, sometimes, Dreams are a Direct Route to
    Reality.

The Isle of Love was as Near as a Sigh;
Eager, our Anticipation was High.
We were Joyous as our Ship rolled over the Waves.
Lifted up, we were Buoyant for many a Day.

Alas, the awaited Isle was in View.
You held me Close, as I Gazed at You.
The Scene before us should Not have been a Surprise.
While many were Happy, others had Tearful Eyes.

For many, the Reward was Worth their Wait,
And far Exceeded anything they could Anticipate.
For others, the Reward had been all too Brief,
Like shifting Sand beneath their Feet.

Let us Drift and Float for a long, long While,
In the Direction of that Fleeting Isle.
We may Sail into many Sunsets in the Sunshine Ship,
And we'll both be Losers.....if we Miss the Trip.

Chapter 8

King of Kings - Faith Speaking
Collection

ARE YOU REALLY A CHRISTIAN?

Are you Really a Christian, do your "Words" and
　　"Music" Match?
When the Lord entered by your Heart's Door, did
　　you Remember to Close the Latch?

Did you Close your Eyes, to your Wrong Ways
　　to Live for Him...all your Days?
Or did you leave Ajar the Door so Willful Sin
　　could Enter In?

Do you try to Justify your Lifestyle to serve Him in
　　Name Only, while Leading others Astray by not
　　Living Holy?
Do you Grieve the Holy Spirit letting Carnal words
　　Slip from your Stunned Lips?

Did Jesus give His "All" for You... or did He hold
　　Something Back?
Would you like to make Amends Today?
Do be Ready, for He is Coming Back!

DID YOU KNOW JESUS, THE CHILD?

Mary, to Joseph, was Betrothed
When an Angel to Mary Spoke.
She was to bear Jesus, the Child,
For God's Love on Mary did Smile.

Jesus was to be the Saviour of All Mankind.
Great Esteem in Mary God did Find.
Jesus was Destined to become a Great Man;
This little Jewish Babe, the Son of God and Mary, in
    Bethlehem.

***

He was Born one Still and Special Night.
Shepherds sent by Angels, joined His Earthly Father,
    Joseph, in the Starlight.
In a Manger, in a Stable, in a Bed of Fresh Straw,
The Animals Welcomed Him and Saw
There, the Lowliest of Births,
As He Came to be on Earth.
The Wise Men Traveled from Afar,
Guided by a Single Star.

He was Human First,
As He Dwelt among Us.
A Crown He was to Gain,
After He had Endured the Pain.
Jesus, The Child, held all Living Things in Awe.
Each Plant and Bird with a Unique Fascination He Saw.
He spoke of God's Wondrous and Manifold Works.
He brought Glory to God through Verse after Verse.

He Recited Bible Prophecies at an Early Age.
Afraid, Old Men kept Silent, and, some Less Fearful,
    were Filled with Rage.

They Marveled, could He be the Messiah, from Heaven
    Sent
By God, in all His Magnificence?
God on High was Glorified;
Holy Words Ascended from The Child.
Who was this Jesus, the Child,
Unlike any Other in Wisdom, yet so Sweet, Loving and
    Mild?

He soon found Life to be Bittersweet and Unrelenting,
And Reacted with Intensity to the Backbreaking Toil of
    Men and Women.
He helped His Mother, Mary, as she Labored in the
    Fields, and Drew Water,
And Worked and did Chores for the Carpenter, Joseph,
    His Father.
Mary sewed all His Garments of Homespun White
    Linen.
He Stood Out in a Crowd, no Matter how Many were In
    It.
With the Rabbis, in the Temple, Jesus Spent much of the
    Day.
When Mary would come to Look for Him, He wanted to
    Stay.

Mary came to see the World in a new Light, a
    Fascination.
Jesus, The Child, became an Illumination.

DID YOU KNOW JESUS, THE MAN?

He traveled over many Paths, throughout the Land,
Healing the Lame and Blind, Helping every Man
In Need, and Preaching Salvation
To the Israel Nation.

Jesus is The Way, no man Cometh unto the Father,
    but by Him.
Through Him only can we receive Forgiveness of Sin.
By Satan, Jesus the Man was also Tempted to Sin.
He Triumphantly Rejected, through God, Satan's
    attempts at Him.

Jesus, the Man, preached The Sermon on the Mount,
    the Beatitudes, and when
Performing Miracles, proved He was the Son of God
    to Men.
He turned Water to Wine, and Walked on Water.
His faithful Friends, His Followers, were called the
    Twelve Apostles.
He Tamed the Angry Seas, and the Winds Obeyed.
He Spent much Time Alone, and to God He Prayed.
From Five Loaves and Two Fishes He fed the
    Multitudes.
There was even Food left Over, that was Not
    Consumed.
Every Knee shall Bow, every Tongue shall Confess
Glory to God and His Righteousness.

He Taught us to Forgive Seventy times Seven,
For such is the Teaching of the Kingdom of Heaven.
From the Story of the Good Samaritan to the Last
    Supper, to Mary Magdalene,
Jesus, the Man, taught Men to Pray to the God they
    had Not yet Seen.

DID YOU KNOW JESUS, THE SAVIOUR?

Men Resented Jesus' claimed Relationship to God,
the Father.
They were Vicious in their Verbal Attacks, and His
Story they Tried to Alter.
There was No Case Against Him that the Scoffers
could Bring,
And the Excited Crowds, that Sought Him, Still
Believed.
The Chief Priests and Pharisees Arranged a Mock
Trial.
In their Corruption, Jesus, the Saviour, was Defiled.
Jesus, the Saviour, Transformed Civilization.
For the Generation of Man He Bought the Plan of
Salvation.
With His Blood He Became Our Substitute.
He Paid the Price for All, even Those of Ill Repute.

Because He was.....
Human,
A Man,
He Experienced Great Trepidation.
Jesus, the Saviour, Suffered Unsurpassed Pain and
Degradation.
His Fate, as Prophesied, was in the Hands of an Evil
Throng.
Jesus, the Saviour, was Blameless and had done No
Wrong.
Jesus, the Good Shepherd, Gave His Life for His
Sheep,
While His Loving Mother, Mary, did Weep.

Jesus, according to Scripture, Arose the Third Day
and Appeared to Man.
They Recognized Him by the Nailprints in His
Hands.

Jesus, the Saviour, Ascended, His Mission on Earth
     Complete,
and Sits on the Right Hand of God, as Our
     Intercessor, within Everyone's Reach.
Behold, He is Standing at Heaven's Door,
And He Speaks, "Go and Sin No More."
"Forgive them, Father, for they Know Not what They
     Do."
Do you Hear Him Now, Speaking to You?

DOES GOD NEED ANOTHER SOPRANO?

Does God need another Soprano, is there any room
    for me in His Choir Loft?
Could He use another Voice to sing Low, Humble
    and Soft?

.....or Loudly sing Praise to the Trinity, the
Three-in-One, to His Holy Name?
To sing to the Creator of Earth and Mankind, the
    Skies, Wind and the Falling Rain?

Could He use another Voice to Proclaim His Deity?
Or to Thank Him for His Love and to Ask Him what
    he Sees in Me?

......to sing with Thanksgiving to Jesus, His Son, for
    His Sacrifice for You and Me,
to echo Calvary's Message
    when Jesus hung upon the Tree?

Does God need another Soprano, for a Trio or a
    Duet.....is there any room for Me?
Or must the Songs within me be Silent... was this why
    Jesus died for You and Me?

THE SINGLE MAN'S PRAYER
- JESUS IS THE BRIDEGROOM -

Oh, Lord, may this little Poem Impart to Others a better
   Understanding
Of how your Philosophy impacts the Millennial
   Man.......in Times Demanding.
You know I'm Saving myself for my Wife, even
   though I may Never Marry.
I'll Not Regret this Choice, because Jesus, my Sins, in
   His Great Love has Carried.

When your Heart Belongs to God, your Body is Not
   your Own.
Jesus bought it on the Cross, and it belongs to Him,
   Alone.
To save Myself for my Wife, Someday,
Seems Small, Compared to the price Jesus Paid.

I'll share a Date with a Lady, but my Body is my
   Own,
And Lord, I Pray there's someone Saving herself for
   Me, Alone.
I Didn't always Believe, you Know I made Mistakes
   along the Way;
But that was in the Past, before Jesus' Grace I found,
   that Wonderful Day.

Even though I may Never Marry, the Bible says that
   Jesus is the Bridegroom!
This Message is so much more Poignant when one
   Considers the Empty Tomb.
Jesus, the Bridegroom, will Return for his Bride, the
   Church, at that Meeting in the Sky.
I want to Keep myself Spotless for You, Lord; I want
   to see You by and By!

THE SINGLE WOMAN'S PRAYER
- JESUS IS THE BRIDEGROOM -

Oh Lord, may this little Poem Impart to Others a
better Understanding
Of how your Philosophy impacts the Millennial
Woman.......in Times Demanding.
You know I'm Saving myself for my Husband, even
though I may Never Marry.
I'll Not Regret this Choice because Jesus, my Sins, in
His Great Love has Carried.

When your Heart Belongs to God, your Body is Not
your Own.
Jesus bought it on the Cross, and it belongs to Him,
Alone.
To save Myself for my Husband, Someday,
Seems small, Compared to the price Jesus Paid.

I'll share a Date with a Gentleman, but my Body is
my Own,
And Lord, I Pray there's someone Saving himself for
Me, Alone.
I didn't always Believe; you Know I made mistakes
Along the Way;
But that was in the Past, before Jesus' Grace I found,
that Wonderful Day.

Even though I may Never Marry, the Bible says that
Jesus is the Bridegroom!
This Message is so much more Poignant, when one
Considers the Empty Tomb.
Jesus, the Bridegroom, will Return for his Bride, the
Church, at that Meeting in the Sky.
I want to Keep myself Spotless for you, Lord; I want
to see You by and By!

THE TALKS WE USED TO SHARE

Seeing You Yesterday with Your Friends
Reminded Me of the Talks we used to Share.
How I Wished the Day would End
And You would Join Me in Evening Prayer.

You went to Sleep, Forgetting the Day
As quickly as the Sunset Disappeared.
Replaced by My Tears, which were the Rain,
You Didn't Notice, as I Feared.

I Watched you Sleep and Longed to Touch your
    Brow.
Spilling Moonlight on Your Pillow,
I Waited, Longing to Touch Down.
Instead, I Whispered it in the Willow.

So Many times I've Missed your Company.
My Love Rushes to you in the Mountain Streams,
Yet your Life goes on Without Me.
Don't you Know you <u>Are</u> the World to Me?

Wrapping you in Warm Sunshine on a Cold Day
I'm Trying to Tell you - I'm All Around You.
In the Fresh, Green Grass in the Month of May
I Send Nature's Fresh Scent to Surround You.

When Your Heart is Heavy with Sorrow
And You're so Sad and Alone, Don't Despair.
You Feel as if there's No Tomorrow.
Remember, I Know, for I have Been There.

As Surely as the Birds sing Love Songs, Child of
    Mine, Please know I have Loved You since Before
    Your Birth and that I Feel your Every Emotion.

May the Promises, in the Book of Life, Remind You that I, too, Once Lived and Walked on Earth And of My Father who Made the Oceans.

WHERE IS GOD?

I've Heard it Said that God is Anywhere We Are;
In the Meadow, on a Hill, in the Distance, No Matter
    how Far.
Some Find a Nearness to God while Surveying His
    Creation,
or Seeking Reverence within His
    Sanctuary.

Wherever you Are, if it is Communion with God you
    are Seeking,
He will be There with you if you Come to Him
    Believing.
Put Aside all Distractions
And Meet with God to Receive Satisfaction.

We Must be in the Right Place, at the Right Time,
To Receive from God a Satisfied Mind.
We must Push Pleasure into the Background
To Derive the Most from the God we have Found.

WHO MADE MAN, PERFECT MAN?

Who made Man, Perfect Man?
With his Sense of Hearing, Touch, Speech and Sight,
Limbs to Walk, a Heart that Beats with Life?
Who made Man, Perfect Man?
Do you Think you Can?
Not I.
Who made the Birds that Fly?
So Graceful as they take to the Heavens in their
    Flight.
Who made the Birds that Fly?
Would you Care to Try?
Not I.
The Flea, the Elephant, the Ant.
Do you Think they just happened by Chance?
The Elegant Ostrich, the Peacock so Proud, the
    Spotted Tiger,
Would you Care to Make Either?

"Nonsense" you Say
As you Wave me Away;
"Of Course there is a Creator.
Doesn't everyone Believe in our Maker?
Then who made the Sun and the Rain,
And who Divided the Night from the Day?
What about the Snow on the Hill,
And the View from My Window, on a Morning
    Still?"

No, Dear Friend, there are the Skeptics, those that
    Reject.
Dare we Doubt the Wind - as we See it's Effects?
By Faith, Believe, is all God asked, and the Angels on
    High
Will Rejoice and His Majesty will Fill the Sky!

The Oceans, the Rushing Rivers, and Streams,
The Forests, Deserts, Stars and Moonbeams
Proclaim the Lord on Every Hand;
Everywhere I see Him throughout the Land.

The Winds that Blow,
The Flowers that Grow,
A Mighty Hand must Make it So.
Who made Man, Perfect Man?
And what of the Soul?
Do you Think you Can?
Not I.

Chapter 9

Tribute to Princess Diana
Collection

A TRIBUTE TO PRINCESS DIANA
- The Pearl -

She was our Fairy-Tale Princess, a Pearl of Great
    Price.
Happiness Transfused her; the Smile of a Child
    Sufficed.
Her Aura Illuminated the Entire World.
Her Mystique Enriched the Priceless Pearl.

Compassion, Worn with Grace and Dignity, was her
    Dazzling Gown.
Her Deep and Abiding Love for her Sons, was her
    Sparkling Crown.

Cloaked in Passion for the World's Ills,
Such as Mere Mortals have Seldom Shown.
She Reigned Demurely, with Quiet Splendor;
The Hearts of the People was her Throne.

With Loyalty, her Mission was Remedy for Desperate
    Causes.
With Empathy, she Embraced others' Lifetime
    Losses.
With a Gentle Spirit, she Approached all her Days.
In Royalty, the Beloved Princess was thus Arrayed.

She took us to a New Height;
What a Magnificent Sight!

IN PRINCESS DIANA'S HONOR
- THE ROSES -

My Heart, Heavy and Filled with Sorrow,
Longs to lay these Flowers at the Gates of England,
and Weep.

Please Accept the Roses in Her Honor......
May She, in the Next Life, find Eternal Peace.

About the Author

Peggy Aston, a daughter of the South, was born in Paducah, Kentucky. A Michigan resident for most of her life since childhood, and career-secretary with Ford Motor Company, she has been writing poetry as a hobby since her late 20's. Her formal works currently number approx. 70.

The lead poem, *The Rivers of My Need*, was written to typify idealistic "true love". Many years later after she became a Christian author as well, she realized that the man in the poem is also the Lord. To quote Peggy, a single parent for many years, "the Lord is the man in the poem and now the man in my life". It is intriguing to reflect on the keynote poem from both human and spiritual perspectives.

Peggy is published in Sparrowgrass, Treasured Poems of America, Summer 1997 (MY DESERT STORM HERO and IN THE VILLAGE CHAPEL) and the forthcoming Voices of the New Century, Summer 1999 (ONLY A FORTNIGHT AGO and TRIBUTE TO PRINCESS DIANA, i.e., THE PEARL and THE ROSES).

SURVIVAL and MY FONDEST DREAM won red roses in WAAM radio's poetry contests for Secretary's Week and Valentine's Day in 1982 and 1983. Peggy's poems have been featured on WAAM's Sunday morning program, Senior Spectrum. MY DESERT STORM HERO was written for her youngest son and went to over 260 troops from lower Michigan stationed in the Gulf, in 1991, as part of a Dom Bakeries local promotion. In conjunction with this effort, she was featured in local newspapers and guest speaker at the Livonia Christian Business & Professional Women's Club.

Known locally as *Poetry Portraits by Peggy*, poetry readings have taken her as guest speaker to Home Shows, Weddings (JOHNNIE, CAN YOU HEAR ME?), and a Memorial Service (CHAR'S LEGACY). Also known locally as *Faith Singing*, she is currently presenting a combination Poetry Reading/Southern Gospel singing program for seniors in nursing/assisted-living residences. She has written poems on request for Retirements,

Birthdays (THE MAN IN THE BROWN BUSINESS SUIT), Graduations (YOU'RE A STAR), Mother's Day (MY MOTHER THE LADY) and Father's Day (MY FAVORITE MAN), Baby Showers (THE ALPHABET LOVE STORY), the Mother of the Bride on the Eve of the Wedding (DAUGHTER OF MINE), among others. ON BEYER'S OLD 4TH FLOOR was written in honor of the nurses on the Maternity Floor there prior to it's recent relocation to St. Joseph's Hospital. DOUBLE X LEX was written for her oldest son for purchase at the Novi Expo Center, January, 1999. THE SEASONS OF OUR LIVES, an inspirational poem about a person who loses their sight as an adult, was donated to the Hope School for Multiple Disabilities, Springfield, Illinois, Valentine's, 1999.